Community Helpers

Fire Fighters

by Dee Ready

Reading Consultant:
George Burke
International Association of Fire Fighters

Bridgestone Books
an Imprint of Capstone Press

Bridgestone Books are published by Capstone Press
151 Good Counsel Drive, P.O. Box 669, Mankato, Minnesota 56002
http://www.capstone-press.com

Library of Congress Cataloging-in-Publication Data
Ready, Dee.
 Fire fighters/by Dee Ready.
 p. cm.—(Community helpers)
 Includes bibliographical references and index.
 Summary: Explains the clothing, tools, schooling, and work of fire fighters.
 ISBN 1-56065-510-0
 1. Fire extinction—Juvenile literature. 2. Fire fighters—Juvenile literature.
[1. Fire extinction. 2. Fire fighters. 3. Occupations.] I. Title. II. Series:
Community helpers (Mankato, Minn.)
TH9148.R43   1997
628.9´25—dc21   96-45424
                                                                      CIP
                                                                       AC

Photo credits
International Stock/Michael Ventura, cover: Mark Bolster, 18
FPG, 4; Mark Reinstein, 6; Spencer Grant, 14
William B. Folsom, 8
Unicorn Stock Photos/Martha McBride, 10; Andre Jenny, 12; Aneal Vohra 16;
 Russell Grundke, 20

Table of Contents

Fire Fighters

Fire fighters are people who are trained to put out fires. They are also the first people to help in a disaster. A disaster destroys things and can kill or hurt people. Being a fire fighter is dangerous work.

What Fire Fighters Do

Fire fighters rescue people and animals in trouble. They are first to help sick or hurt people. They take them to a hospital. Fire fighters put out fires in houses, office buildings, and forests.

What Fire Fighters Wear

Fire fighters wear clothes that help protect them from heat and smoke. They wear special pants and jackets, heavy boots, and gloves. Helmets protect their heads. Air tanks on their backs help them breathe.

Tools Fire Fighters Use

Tools help fire fighters save people from fires. If needed, fire fighters use axes to break down walls. They use crowbars to open doors. They use long hoses to spray water on fires.

What Fire Fighters Drive

Fire fighters drive fire trucks and ambulances. Some fire trucks pump water. Other trucks have ladders that reach people trapped in high places. Ambulances carry hurt people to the hospital.

Fire Fighters and School

Fire fighters must be at least 18 years old. They go to fire fighting school. If they pass special tests, they get a job. They keep learning at the fire station.

Where Fire Fighters Work

Fire fighters work at the fire station. They take turns living there. The fire station is like a house. It has beds and a kitchen. The fire trucks and ambulances are at the fire station, too.

People Who Help Fire Fighters
Fire fighters need other people to help
them do their jobs. Police officers
sometimes help by keeping people
away from the fire. Doctors care for fire
fighters who are hurt on the job.

Fire Fighters Help Others

Fire fighters help everyone in a community. They save people and animals from fire and other disasters. They teach fire safety at schools.

Hands On: Get in Shape

Fire fighters have to be in shape to fight fires. They work out to stay healthy and strong. You can use a bath towel to get in shape, too.

Windmills

1. Hold one end of the towel in each hand. Put the towel behind your head. Keep your arms straight.
2. Bend at the waist to touch your right hand to your left foot.
3. Straighten up and touch your left hand to your right foot.
4. Touch each foot at least 10 times.

Rocking Horses

1. Lie on your stomach on the floor.
2. Bend your knees and hook the towel over your feet.
3. Pull with your arms. This will bring your thighs off the floor.
4. Pull with your feet. This will bring your chest off the floor.
5. Keep rocking as long as you can.

You can also run laps and do sit-ups, push-ups, and jumping jacks.

Words to Know

ambulance (AM-byuh-luhnss)—a vehicle that takes hurt or sick people to a hospital

community (kuh-MEW-nuh-tee)—a group of people who live in the same area

crowbar (KROH-bar)—an iron bar with a flat end

disaster (duh-ZASS-tur)—an event that destroys things and can kill or hurt people

rescue (RESS-kyoo)—to save someone

Read More

Brady, Peter. *Fire Trucks.* Transportation. Mankato, Minn.: Bridgestone Books, 1996.

Saunders-Smith, Gail. *The Fire Station.* Field Trips. Mankato, Minn.: Pebble Books, 1998.

Schomp, Virginia. *If You Were a Firefighter.* New York: Benchmark Books, 1998.

Internet Sites

The Fire FAQ
http://www.cybercid.com/lrfd/firefaq.htm

Fire Safe Kids: The Fire Fighter
http://www. state.il.us/kids/fire/fireman.htm

Index